This story is dedicated to my grandmother; a woman who was the rock
of our family and who was my guardian angel here on earth.
I thank God for allowing her to be a nurturing powerful force in my life.
Thank you grandma, I miss you...............Minnie Pearl Turman.

Library of congress Control Number: 2015907195

ISBN (978-0-692-42920-4)

WindChild Books LLC

Lebra Shawn

Soup for A Gloomy Day

I had never really liked extra cold days.
My feet were numb. My hands were frozen
and felt like a block of ice.
I was already feeling gloomy on account
of the bad day at school.

In class Mrs. Johnson called on me. I didn't know the answer. So, Monisha teased me all day about how I was not smart enough to be in the same class.

I tried to ignore her and pretend it didn't matter but it hurt-it hurt really bad!

117

On the way to music class, the teacher yelled at
me for not hearing when she told the class
to stop at room 117.

And at lunch time, I slipped outside
while running from Craig- it sure made his day !
I guess it's better to wear sneakers than
fancy shoes with ribbons.

Oh Boy! This was not my day.
Now I'm walking home with a
cold face because to top it off,
I lost my favorite scarf that my
grandma bought me.

I felt so alone. I couldn't wait to get to
grandma's house and cry. Just as I pressed
her doorbell a tear rolled from my eye.
But I told myself not to let another fall.
I didn't want grandma to worry.

Grandma opened the door.
Her small apartment was so warm it felt
as though the sun lived there.

Grandma looked at me
and smiled. She had me
put my coat, bag, and
shoes in what seemed like
a special place just for me.

She kept smiling and her smile made me feel
a smile inside. It was as if she knew
I needed it; as if she knew I had a bad day.

"Wash your hands," she said. "I have a special surprise for you." I glowed inside. I rushed to the bathroom, washed my hands and dried them. When I came out, I heard grandma in the kitchen.

I walked in. "Sit down," she said.
At that moment I had forgotten all
the things that happened to me
that day. And even if I hadn't,
I didn't care because it meant
nothing--- Absolutely nothing!

Grandma made my favorite soup;
it sat on the table in a special bowl,
with a special spoon,
on a special place mat,
with buttered bread
and apple cider.

We sat there together eating.
"Feel better now?" she asked.
"Yes Grandma," I said. I felt
better down to the last spoonful.

Grandma let out a big laugh
and hugged me
in a way only grandmas can.

After that we drank hot chocolate
and sat and watched grandma's
favorite show.

Just then grandma looked at me with her
understanding eyes and held my chin in her hand
and said, "You know, sometimes you'll have
those days, but always remember that
You are You; and You are a wonderful
You to be.....Always."

"I will grandma.........I will."

Made in the USA
Columbia, SC
10 September 2020